HAMMERHEAD SHARKS

Anne Welsbacher

Capstone Press
M I N N E A P O L I S

Printed in the United States of America.

Capstone Press • 2440 Fernbrook Lane • Minneapolis, MN 55447

Editorial Director   John Coughlan
Managing Editor   John Martin
Production Editor   James Stapleton
Copy Editor   Thomas Streissguth

Library of Congress Cataloging-in-Publication Data

Welsbacher, Anne, 1955-
    Hammerhead sharks / by Anne Welsbacher.
      p. cm. -- (Sharks)
    Includes bibliographical references (p.) and index.
    ISBN 1-56065-270-5
    1. Hammerhead sharks--Juvenile literature.
    [1. Hammerhead sharks. 2. Sharks.] I. Title.
    II. Series: Welsbacher, Anne, 1955- Sharks.
QL638.95.S7W45 1996
597'.31--dc20   95-7125
                                                            CIP

99 98 97 96 95   6 5 4 3 2 1

Table of Contents

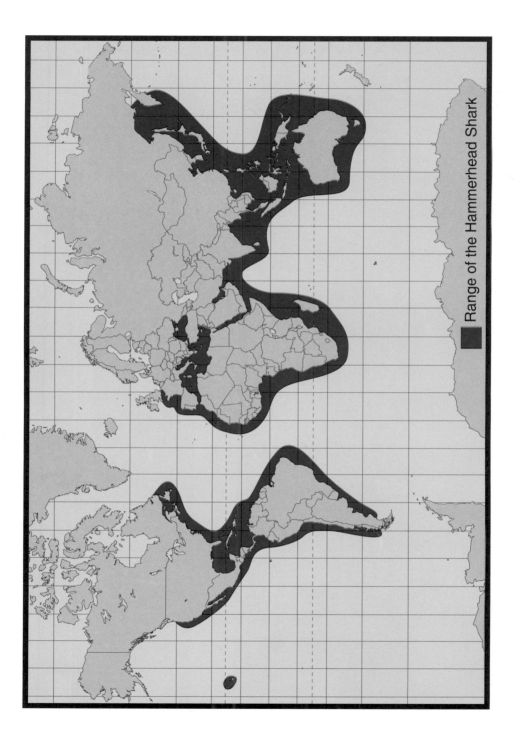

Range of the Hammerhead Shark

Facts about Hammerhead Sharks

Scientific names: There are nine **species** of hammerheads, eight in one **genus,** *Sphyrna*. The largest is the great hammerhead, *Sphyrna mokarran*. One hammerhead, the winghead, is usually put in a separate genus, *Eusphyra blochii*.

Description: All hammerheads have heads shaped like a hammer, shovel, or letter T. They have round eyes and nostrils at each end of the hammer. The widest hammer belongs to the winghead. The smallest belongs to the bonnethead.

Length: The smallest species, the bonnetheads, are 3 to 3.5 feet (90 to 105 centimeters). The largest hammerheads are the great hammerhead, the common hammerhead, and the scalloped hammerhead. They range from 10 to 15 feet (3 to 5 meters) long. Great hammerheads may reach 20 feet (6.1 meters).

Weight: The great hammerhead weighs up to 1,500 pounds (680 kilograms). One weighing 1,000 pounds (454 kilograms) is considered big.

Color: Dark olive, brownish, or gray above, and lighter, sometimes white, below.

Location: Around the world in warm ocean waters, fairly near land. The winghead is limited to the Pacific Ocean near India and Indonesia.

Chapter 1

A Mighty Strange Shark

One look tells you how this shark got its name. Its head is shaped like the head of a hammer, making it one of the strangest-looking fish in the sea.

From the side, the hammerhead looks like a standard shark, though the top part of its tail fin is longer than most sharks'. If it turns its head, you'll see that its head is hammer-shaped. Or you might call it T-shaped.

The front of its head seems to have been stretched out sideways, making two flattened **lobes**. The shark's eyes and nostrils are on the ends of the lobes.

There are nine different types of hammerheads. Some are small, others are huge. Some can kill people, but most are harmless.

The heads of some hammerheads look more like shovels or old-fashioned bonnets. The heads of others look like axes. Still others have heads that look like boomerangs.

Using Their Heads

The hammer-shaped heads help hammerheads see and catch prey. The sense organs that let them see and smell are right out there in front. Nothing gets in the way.

Hammerheads have a special muscle to move their heads up and down, like an elevator, and from side to side. Because its mouth is tucked way back under the hammer, the moving head helps the hammerhead eat.

A school of fish scatters at the approach of a scalloped hammerhead.

Sometimes these sharks use their hammers like hammers. One scientist watched a hammerhead shark use its hammer to hold down and strike its prey.

Hammerheads don't have bone in their heads. In fact, sharks don't have any bone in

The great hammerhead swims in warm coastal waters. This one was found off the Bahamas, an Atlantic Ocean island group.

their bodies. Their skeletons are made of **cartilage**. Cartilage is softer than bone but still stiff. You have cartilage in your nose, kneecap, and outer ears.

Where They Swim

Hammerheads swim in warm, shallow and coastal waters throughout the world. Smaller hammerheads often swim into water that is partly fresh, as in the mouths of rivers.

The three largest hammerheads have the broadest range. The great and the common hammerheads swim off the warmer coasts of both northern and southern continents. Scalloped hammerheads swim in warm, tropical waters near the equator.

Chapter 2

Little Hammerheads and Big Hammerheads

There are nine species of hammerhead, and they vary greatly in size.

Many Sizes

The two smallest hammerheads grow no larger than 3 to 3.5 feet (90 to 105 centimeters) long. Their hammers curve around their front. They look more like bonnets than hammers. These sharks are called bonnetheads.

The smallest of these is the scalloped bonnethead *(Sphyrna corona)*. Its bonnet looks scalloped from above. It's ash-colored on top and white below. The bonnethead, sometimes called the shovelhead *(Sphyrna tiburo)*, is nearly as small. It's mouse-gray above and lighter below.

The scoophead *(Sphyrna media)* and the smalleye *(Sphyrna tudes)* are mouse-gray, too, and grow to about 3.5 feet (105 centimeters).

The rare West African white fin *(Sphyrna couardi)* grows to 7 feet (2.1 meters) and is the same color.

The Big Ones

Only three of the hammerhead species are large enough to be dangerous. Fortunately, the teeth of these large sharks are so small and weak that they are useless in attacking. Only their bulk makes these sharks dangerous.

The three largest hammerheads look quite alike. Only small differences in the shape of the front edge of the hammer make them different.

The largest, called the great hammerhead, is 12 to 15 feet (3.6 to 4.5 meters) long and may reach 20 feet (6.1 meters). Its color is dark

The great hammerhead has small teeth but a large body that can be dangerous to divers.

olive green. Its head is T-shaped and almost flat. From above, it looks like a rectangle with eyes. The great hammerhead's big **dorsal**, or back, fin is closer to its head than most sharks' dorsal fins are.

The scalloped, also called the bronze, hammerhead *(Sphyrna lewini)* is olive brown,

This scalloped hammerhead roams off the Galapagos Islands, in the Pacific Ocean.

with charcoal-colored tips on its fins. Its head is rounded, with an indentation in the middle of the wavy front edge. It gets to be as long as 11 feet (3.4 meters).

The common, or smooth, hammerhead (*Sphyrna zygaena*) also has a scalloped head. It does not have the indentation like the scalloped hammerhead does. Olive-gray in color, it rarely gets to be more than about 13 feet (4 meters) long.

Strangest of All

The weirdest-looking of all the hammerheads is the winghead *(Eusphyra blochii)*. It looks like a fish with wings on its head. Its hammer looks like a boomerang because the wings sweep back.

Sometimes the winghead's hammer is equal in width to half the shark's length. The winghead grows to about 5 or 6 feet (1.5 or 1.8 meters) long and its head may be close to 3 feet (90 centimeters) wide.

The winghead can be found in tropical waters in the Red Sea, the Persian Gulf, off the Philippines and Malaysia, and northwest of Australia. It is not dangerous to people.

Chapter 3

Hammerheads
in School

Most sharks are loners. They swim and hunt alone. Scalloped hammerheads and bonnetheads, however, swim in groups or schools.

They seem to have social systems, like ants or people. While they swim together, for example, the larger fish swim on the outside edges of the schools. The biggest fish may be the leader.

Scientists don't know why hammerheads swim in schools. They don't need the protection. Nor do they swim together to feed. In fact, when they go after prey, they go alone.

Body Language

Bonnetheads have patterns to their behavior. They make certain movements over and over again. These movements, called "body language," mean things to other sharks. People may someday figure out what these movements mean.

The bonnetheads shake their heads, they swim rapidly back and forth, and they circle around as if chasing their tails. They will arch their backs, lower their tails, or raise their heads in a "hunch."

Sometimes they do wild stunts while they swim. They jerk up and down suddenly. They corkscrew, twisting all the way around while swimming fast in a circle. A corkscrewing hammerhead sometimes runs right into another hammerhead.

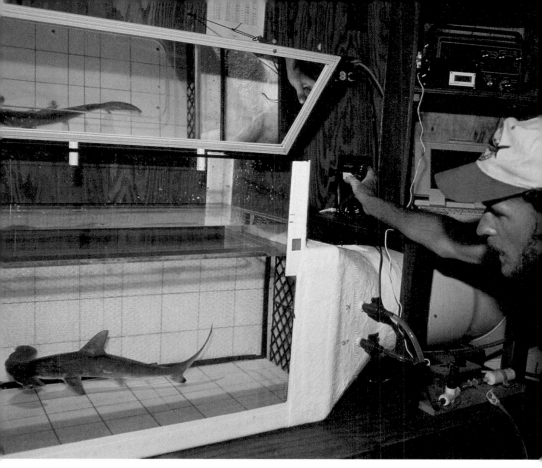

A scientist examines young hammerheads in a lab in Hawaii. Measurement devices reveal the sharks *metabolism*, or life system.

Predicting Behavior

Bonnetheads swim in schools that number in the thousands. Scientists have studied bonnethead schools. They think some sharks have behavior that can be predicted. In the

A hammerhead pup lies on top of the birth sac—the part of the mother that carries the young.

same situations, they can be counted on to do the same things.

Unfortunately, the bigger sharks can't be kept together and studied like bonnetheads can.

It will be a long time before we know if the behavior of all sharks can be predicted.

Mating Habits

Most sharks, including most hammerheads, are with other sharks only when they are mating. Scientists have seen male hammerheads ramming or even biting females. They think this is mating behavior.

Male hammerheads use **claspers** to mate with females. Claspers are like extra fins on the male's stomach, or **ventral**, side. The claspers are used to hold onto the female. The male also uses them to put sperm into an opening on the female's ventral side.

The Young Ones

Unlike most fish and some other sharks, hammerheads do not lay their eggs in the water. The eggs stay inside the female, where they hatch. The young continue to develop there. The females give birth to live young called pups.

A school of scalloped hammerheads gather near the surface.

Small bonnetheads have 8 to 12 pups, each of them about 12 inches (30 centimeters) long at birth. The much larger great hammerhead can have 20 to 40 pups, each about 2 feet (60 centimeters) long at birth.

When hammerheads are born, their hammers are soft. This allows them to pass safely out of their mother. As they grow, the hammer hardens.

Young and small hammerheads are more likely then older and larger ones to be found in shallow bays. They generally ignore people.

Chapter 4

That Weird Head

W hy is the head of a hammerhead shaped the way it is? Scientists have several ideas.

Some scientists believe that the strange shape of the hammerhead shark's head is an experiment in **evolution**. The shape "evolved" over time because it helped the shark survive in some way.

Some experiments in evolution end with the animal disappearing, or becoming **extinct**. In Ireland, for example, there once lived a type of elk that had antlers 15 feet (4.5 meters) wide. That was too wide for the animal to move through the forests, however, and it became extinct.

Putting the Hammer to Work

The shape of a hammerhead's hammer may be helpful in swimming and diving. It might give extra lift like the wings of an airplane. The hammer may also help the shark to make tight, quick turns when chasing food.

The Nostrils

The hammerhead's nostrils are right out in front, even in front of the eyes. A hammerhead isn't likely to miss the scent of anything.

Sharks have a good sense of smell anyway. They can smell blood when there's only one tiny drop of blood in one million drops of water. And they can smell it from a quarter of a mile (400 meters) away.

On a great hammerhead, the two nostrils may be as much as 3 feet (90 centimeters) apart. With nostrils set far apart like this, a hammerhead can smell prey first with one side of its head and then with the other. The two different scents might tell the shark where its prey is.

The wide head and round eyes of the hammerhead help this fish to see its prey better than most other sharks.

Eyes and Ears

Eyesight is not important to most sharks until they get quite close to their prey. But hammerheads, with their round eyes on the ends of their hammers, can probably see better than other sharks. The large space between

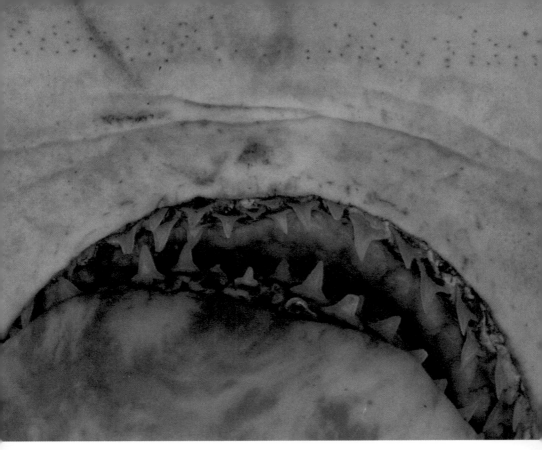

The ampullae of Lorenzini sit along the jaws of the hammerhead. This organ can sense electrical signals given off by the shark's prey.

their eyes helps them figure out just how far away their prey is.

Hammerheads' eyes have extra protection, an extra eyelid called a **nictitating membrane**.

This eyelid closes over the eye when danger threatens. It also closes when they bite into their prey, just in case the prey bites back. The shark can still see through this special eyelid.

Sharks' ears pick up regular sounds, but they also have another kind of sense organ. This is a thin strip that runs the length of each side of the body. Called the **lateral line**, this is a strip of sensory cells that picks up sounds that are too low for ears to hear. Sharks use the lateral line to "hear" thrashing fish and other distant vibrations.

Suppertime Signals

All sharks have special sense organs on their heads called **ampullae of Lorenzini**. They are tiny pores around the sharks' jaws. Ampullae were small bottles in ancient Rome, and the man who discovered these strange shark organs was named Lorenzini.

These great hammerheads may be sensing a stingray buried under the sandy bottom.

The hammer on a hammerhead has a wide, flat surface on the underside. And they have more of these ampullae than other sharks.

The ampullae sense the electrical signals given off by all living creatures. When any animal muscle moves, it gives off signals. If a creature is wounded, its signals are even stronger. With their ampullae, hammerheads can even find stingrays buried under sand.

Sharks can sense electrical signals better than other animals can, and hammerheads can sense these signals better than other sharks.

Chapter 5
Hunting and Eating

Hammerheads eat mainly other fish and such creatures as crabs and lobsters. Bonnetheads eat shrimp.

Hammerheads also eat other hammerheads. One naturalist caught a 14-foot (4.3-meter) hammerhead that had in its belly parts or all of six other hammerheads. Two of the swallowed sharks were whole.

Stingray Prey

Hammerheads eat fish called skates and also rays, which are related to sharks. Their

Divers use tough chain suits to protect themselves from sharks.

usual prey are stingrays, which have sharp, poisonous stingers in their tails.

Almost every hammerhead ever caught or seen has had a stingray's barb hanging off it. One hammerhead had 96 barbs stuck in its mouth and head.

Hammerheads use their wide heads to hunt for stingrays. They cruise along the bottom of the ocean. They swing their heads back and forth like minesweepers or giant metal detectors.

Teeth

The larger hammerheads are on the list of dangerous sharks. But hammerheads have very weak teeth and are not likely to take large bites out of people.

The great hammerhead has teeth with saw, or **serrated**, edges. The scalloped hammerhead has smooth-edged teeth. The common hammerhead has teeth that are smooth when the animal is young and slightly serrated later.

Hammerheads have several rows of teeth in their jaws. But they are small and weak teeth, compared to those of other sharks. This makes the hammerhead less dangerous to humans than other shark species.

Hammerheads have several rows of teeth in their jaws. Only the front row of teeth stands up and is used for eating. When a shark loses a front tooth, another tooth moves up from

A diver replaces a young hammerhead in the ocean.

behind to replace it. This new tooth, full
grown, sometimes moves into place in only 24
hours.

The Remora

The remora is a small fish that appears to be upside down. Its back fin is a sucker that allows it to attach itself to a much bigger fish, usually a shark. After going along for an effortless ride, the remora may drop off, attracted to another surface—a boat, a rock, or another fish. The shark rarely eats its passenger.

Chapter 6

Hammerheads and Humans

Sailors in the sixteenth century thought that it was very bad luck if they saw a hammerhead shark. Today, especially for fishermen, it can be good luck.

The larger hammerheads are good game fish. They can give a mighty tug on the fishing line, but they don't fight for very long.

The largest great hammerhead ever caught weighed 991 pounds (about 45 kilograms). It was caught off Florida.

To follow the shark's movements, scientists feed it a tracking device.

Hammerhead Attack

Large hammerheads usually stay in deep water. But they have been known to chase prey into the shallow water where people swim and sail. They have been accused of unprovoked attacks on people and boats. Several attacks have occurred in the waters off Florida.

Hammerheads in Aquariums

Because hammerheads look so interesting, many people have tried to keep them in aquariums for visitors to see. But the larger hammerheads do not live well in captivity. In fact, most captured hammerheads have died only a few days after they were caught.

Glossary

ampullae of Lorenzini–fluid-filled sacs in sharks that can sense vibrations and help sharks "hear"

cartilage–a stiff but bendable body tissue. Sharks have a skeleton made of cartilage instead of bone.

claspers–a pair of organs located on the abdomen on a male shark, used for mating. They look like extra fins.

dorsal–located on the back of a shark, as dorsal fins

evolution–the long process of change in animals and plants that gradually creates different species

extinct–gone forever

genus–a group of living things with some traits in common

lateral line–a row of special sensory cells along the side of a shark. It senses motion in the water.

lobes–rounded sections of a body part

nictitating membrane–a special protective eyelid found in hammerhead sharks and in some other animals

serrated–saw-toothed

species–a certain kind of animal or plant. Usually only creatures within one species mate with each other.

ventral–located on the bottom side, or stomach, of a shark, as ventral fins

About the Author

Anne Welsbacher is publications director at the Science Museum of Minnesota. She writes science articles for various publications and is a playwright.

To Learn More

Blassingame, Wyatt. *Wonders of Sharks.* New York: Dodd, Mead, and Co., 1984.

Cerullo, Mary M. *Sharks: Challengers of the Deep.* New York: Cobblehill Books, 1993.

Freedman, Russel. *Sharks.* New York: Holiday House, 1985.

Langley, Andrew. *The World of Sharks.* New York: Bookwright Press, 1987.

Index